Alone and Not Alone

ALONE AND NOT ALONE

Ron Padgett

Coffee House Press
Minneapolis
2015

Coffee House Press books are available to the trade through our primary distributor, Consortium Book Sales & Distribution, cbsd.com or (800) 283-3572. For personal orders, catalogs, or other information, write to: info@coffeehousepress.org.

Coffee House Press is a nonprofit literary publishing house. Support from private foundations, corporate giving programs, government programs, and generous individuals helps make the publication of our books possible. We gratefully acknowledge their support in detail in the back of this book.

Visit us at coffeehousepress.org.

LIBRARY OF CONGRESS CATALOGING-IN-PUBLICATION DATA
Padgett, Ron, 1942–
[Poems. Selections]
Alone and not alone / Ron Padgett.
pages cm
ISBN 978-1-56689-401-2
I. Title.
PS3566.A32A6 2014
811'.54—dc23

PRINTED IN THE UNITED STATES
FIRST EDITION | FIRST PRINTING

ACKNOWLEDGMENTS
Some of the poems in this volume were published in *Aphros, Cerise Press, Coconut, Connotation Press, Court Green, Courtland Review, For the One Fund Boston* (Granary Books), *Hanging Loose, Poem-a-Day* (Academy of American Poets), *Sentence, Tablet, Test Centre,* and *Upstreet.*

for Wayne

Contents

Alone and Not Alone

What Poem

What poem
were you thinking of,
my dear,
as you breezed out the door
in your long coat fur-tipped
at the top?
What animal
once wore that fur
and licked it
with a long, raspy tongue
that lolled to one side
in the afternoon shade?
If only you too
could lope across
the Serengeti Plain
and grab something
in your powerful jaws,
instead of pausing
at the door and saying,
as if in afterthought,
"Write a poem
while I'm out."

The Roman Numerals

It must have been hard
for the Romans to multiply
—I don't mean reproduce,
but to do that computation.

Step inside a roman numeral
for a moment, a long one
such as MDCCLIX. Look
at the columns and pediments
and architraves: you cannot move them,
but how beautiful they are
and august! However, try to multiply
MDCCCLXIV by MCCLVIII.

How did they do it?

I asked this question some years ago
and never found an answer
because I never looked for one,
but it is pleasant,
living with this question.

Perhaps the Romans weren't good at math,
unlike the Arabs, who arrived
with baskets of numerals, plenty
for everyone. We still have
more than we need today.

I have a 6 and a 7 that,
when put side by side, form my age.

Come to think of it,
I'd rather be LXVII.

Butterfly

Chaung Tzu wrote about the man
who dreamed he was a butterfly
and when he woke up
wondered if he weren't now
a butterfly dreaming he was a man.

I love this idea
though I doubt that Chaung Tzu
really thought that a man would think
he is a butterfly,

for it's one thing to wake up
from a dream in the night
and another to spend your whole life
dreaming you are a man.

I have spent my whole life
thinking I was a boy, then a man,
also a person and an American
and a physical entity and a spirit
and maybe a little bit butterfly.
Maybe I should be more butterfly,

that is, lurch into a room
with bulging eyes and big flapping wings
that throw a choking powder
onto people who scream and fall dead,

almost. For I would rescue them
with the celestial music of my beauty
and my utter harmlessness,
my ætherial disregard of what they are.

Reality

Reality has a transparent veneer
that looks exactly like the reality beneath it.
If you look at anything,
your hands, for instance, and wait,
you will see it. Then
it will flicker and vanish,
though it is still there.
You must wait a day or two
before attempting to see it again,
for each attempt uses up
your current allotment of reality viewing.
Meanwhile there is a coffee shop
where you can sit and drink coffee,
and where you will be tempted
to look down at the cup and see
the transparent veneer again,
but that is only because you are overstimulated.
Do not order another cup. Or do.
It will have no effect on the veneer.

Sometimes the veneer becomes detached
and moves slightly away from reality,
as when you look up and see a refrigerator
in refrigerator heaven, cold and quiet.
But then the veneer snaps back
to its former position and vanishes.
This is a normal occurrence—
do not be alarmed by it.

Instead, drive to the store
and buy something
that looks like milk, return
home and place it in the refrigerator.

Days go by, years go by, people
grow older and die, surrounded,
if they are lucky, by younger people
who do not know what to do
with feelings whose veneers
have slipped to the side, far
to the side, and are staying there
too long. But eventually they will grow hungry
and tired, and an image of dinner and bed
will float in like a leaf
that fell from who knows where, and sleep.

The Chinese Girl

When I order a coffee that is half-real, half-decaf, with half-and-half, the women behind the counter invariably give me a blank look and wait for something to come clear in their heads, and when it doesn't I repeat, slowly, my order, gesturing with my fingers to demonstrate the half-real, then the half-decaf part. When it finally registers on them and they fill the cup, I point to the carton of half-and-half. Then one of the two—they work in pairs—asks, "Shu gah?"

However, the youngest of the morning crew of five understands better than the other four, so I always hope to have her wait on me, not only because of her better English but because she is the cutest. Of course not all Chinese girls look the same, but descriptions of them tend to sound the same, so I'm not sure that it would help to say that she has straight black hair, parted in the front and held in place by the bakery uniform's light-green kerchief, a slightly flattened nose, and dark eyes, with a small mole on the right above her top lip. Her modest demeanor lends her an air of innocence. She is what, around eighteen?

I always look forward to seeing her on my weekly visit to the bakery. This morning when I walked slowly along the display case of dazzling muffins, buns, rolls, danishes, and other pastries, trying to decide among them, I heard her voice on the other side, asking, "Can I help you?" Never before had one of the crew left the cash register area to do this.

Concealing my surprise, I asked her, "Are the croissants ready yet?"

"I will see."

When she came back from the kitchen she said, "Five minutes."

"Then I'll have one of these danishes."

"You want small coffee, no? Half-regular, half-decaf, with half-and-half?"

Astonished, I said, "Yes, that's right. You have a good memory."

"I remember *you*," she said, causing my heart to flutter. But my composure returned when she asked, "Shu gah?"

At the register she handed me the change from a five. I took a single and, pointedly ignoring the tip jar, handed it to her, saying "This is for you. *Sheh sheh*."

"Thank you," she said, lowering her eyes and almost imperceptibly drawing back.

I got the signal, so I headed toward an empty table, where I removed the plastic lid from the paper cup and took a bite out of the danish. A band of steam rose from the coffee, like a curtain on a miniature stage. The Chinese girl and I are living in a remote part of China. Our past lives have been erased. She is unspeakably devoted to me and I adore her. We say little, passing our days in a state of calm I could never have imagined.

Smudges

Smattering of gray puffs   rocks are they
large ones but   if you pick them up   light
too light   but fun to lift   and marvel at
they don't make "sense"   they
aren't broken   they are what   you
have laughing in you   almost out
smudges come out   of the rock
you breathe in   and out   the same gray rock
each time as if looped in a cartoon
of a sleeping man   from whom z's
emanate

Smattering of gray puffs   a man is one of them
a cloud   a smudge   a powder of stone
from which a city arises   with people in it
and ideas   that flow toward you and through you
it's too late   it's already happened   to the next you
and the gray smudge   that is your face   turning
into your next face   the one you forget
as soon as it happens   as you fall away
among other smudges that are falling away
smudges and puffs falling away

It Takes Two

My replacement in the universe
is the little tyke who'll soon arrive
and let me be superfluous if
and when I feel like being so.

I don't really mean that.
It's just the openness
of what will or might be,
when what matters most
is the right now of now,
which,
when I draw back and look reveals
an old fool in the foggy bliss
of whatever this morning is.

Straighten up, old thing!
You aren't *that* old and he or she
will reach right up and grasp
some years and break them off
your psyche—what is it? like stardust?
glittering on those tiny tiny fingers.

The First Time

The first time Marcello went outside
the sun and moon were at his side
(his happy mom and happy dad)
(also the happiness known as granddad).
The first time Marcello breathed the outside air
he seemed to like it there.
The first time he got in a car
it zoomed him fast and far
(for such a little guy)
to Brooklyn: "Hi,
Brooklyn!" he didn't shout:
his words were too little to get out.
But clearly in his sleeping face
he felt comfy in the human race.

Circles

Marcello sees
    the sun is yellow.
But then at night
    it's white.
No, that's the moon
    or a white balloon
above his bed—
    wait, it's his head!
Colored circles rise and fall.
    Marcello seems to like them all.

Grandpa Brushed His Teeth

This morning Grandpa brushed his teeth
so hard it knocked Marcello down
but he got back up to watch
Grandpa brush those teeth

Ah Grandpa brushing up and down
with joy he sang almost Glug glug!
The toothpaste tasted excellent
and the brush it zigged and zagged

It's a good thing he has teeth to brush
and that he likes the brushing of them
The only missing ones are Wisdom
and Marcello does not need them

And Grandpa doesn't either
Good-bye to Wisdom teeth and Wisdom
Buon giorno to Marcello
Little toothbrush fellow

Coffee Man

She might be hearing the burbling song of the bird outside, but it is impossible to tell, since she has rolled over and I think gone back to sleep. If I were to say quietly, "Good morning, dear, here is your coffee," she would open her eyes and manage a groggy "Thank you." But when she realizes that I am standing there without coffee, I would forget which tense I'm waiting to lift from the jar with the red lid in the kitchen.

Where Is My Head?

It makes you nervous to think not about death
but about dying and being dead yourself
but when you don't think about it
it doesn't exist,
at least in your universe.
And since that's the universe you happen to be in
you want to stay there:
you have to fix the world
and then save it,
you have to do that one thing
you can't remember what it is
but you know it's there somewhere
like the death you forgot for a moment.

I should have spent my life
meditating so deeply that the thought of death
would be relaxing like a breeze or a feather
but instead I have spent it promising myself
that someday I would go to that special place
in my psyche where the spirit enters and leaves
and make my peace with the beast I call myself.

I hate myself for dying, how
could I have done this!
But all I did was nothing
other than believe that I was actually important!
Everything my mother did proved it.
But when she died she just glided away—

she didn't mind at all.
She didn't think she was important
and she had a farmgirl's view of dying:
chickens do it all the time,
they run around the yard with blood
gushing from where their heads used to be.

I wish I could do that!

In Paris the heads that dropped into the basket
—were they still thinking about the executioner?

Today I am my own executioner.

Survivor Guilt

It's very easy to get.
Just keep living and you'll find yourself
getting more and more of it.
You can keep it or pass it on,
but it's a good idea to keep a small portion
for those nights when you're feeling so good
you forget you're human. Then drudge it up
and float down from the ceiling
that is covered with stars that glow in the dark
for the sole purpose of being beautiful for you,
and as you sink their beauty dims and goes out—
I mean it flies out the nearest door or window,
its whoosh raising the hair on your forearms.
If only your arms were green, you could have two small lawns!
But your arms are just there and you are kaput.
It's all your fault, anyway, and it always has been—
the kind word you thought of saying but didn't,
the appalling decline of human decency, global warming,
thermonuclear nightmares, your own small cowardice,
your stupid idea that you would live forever—
all *tua culpa*. John Phillip Sousa
invented the sousaphone, which is also your fault.
Its notes resound like monstrous ricochets.

But when you wake up, your body
seems to fit fairly well, like a tailored suit,
and you don't look too bad in the mirror.
Hi there, feller!

Old feller, young feller, who cares?
Whoever it was who felt guilty last night,
to hell with him. That was then.

The Young Cougar

The doors swing open and in walks a young cougar wearing white shoes and light-blue socks, come to help his father. "Where do we put this in the registry?" one servant asks another. Or *they* were wearing the shoes and socks.

Radio in the Distance

for Yvonne Jacquette

Beneath the earth covered with men
with snow atop their heads, down
to where it is dark and deep, to where
the big black vibrating blob of wobble
is humming its one and only note, I lie,
orange hair not in the idea of diagonal,
a Betty not composed of vertical fish
or dog with grid-mark cancellations,
but easy as an orchestra of toy atoms
lazy with buzz and fizzle in their drift
as if above this late and lost Manhattan
spread out like a diagram of what we want
from heaven, wherever it is when we think
we know what it is and even when it really is.

Face Value

From a face comes a body an entire body
and from a body everything

but I can't face you
fully
not yet
maybe never

and even if I did or thought I did
how would I know

How would I know
what face value is

From a face comes face value
and from face value a lot of baling wire
—the face scribbled over with dark coils of it

I was born in Kentucky almost
There were no faces there
so I was born elsewhere
from inside a fencepost
to which barbed wire had been affixed
by Frederic Remington

The air was cool, the night calm
and each star had a face
like a movie star's or someone in the family

They too had star quality I thought

but they had statue quality
and then turned sideways
like music blending into fabric and little curtains
along the kitchen windows

attractive kitchen windows

Now you can sit down at this table
and look me square in the eye
and tell me what you've been wanting to
or you can stand up like a photograph on a piano
and sing to me
a song that has no words or music

Which is it? —But

a heavy magnetic force pulls you to the wall
and holds you there

As soon as you get used to it
it lets you go

for a while

and then *your* heavy magnetic force pulls the wall to *you*
and you walk around with a wall stuck to your side
The Wall of Forgetting
it's called

but it's not a wall it's a mirror
that picks your face up off the floor
and whirls it onto a head
that has gone on without you

The Plank and the Screw

There *is* one thing.

In a fishing village on the coast of Norway
an idea came forth and spread
over the country and from there
to the rest of the world, namely
that floating inside the sun was its power source:
a plank and a screw
that had come loose from it,
and as long as they floated around,
never far one from the other,
the sun would continue to burn.

Let's try to imagine how hot it is
one inch from the sun.

Now that we have found it
impossible to imagine
we can go on
to the next thing we do not understand.

Meanwhile, the plank and the screw
continue to float—
the plank is roughly an eight-foot
one-by-ten, the screw a three-inch flathead—
but since there is nothing around them
except burning gas
they are both highly visible.

Many years passed.
Gradually the idea that had come from Norway
became so assimilated into the everyday lives
of people that they never thought of it—
it changed from an idea into people,
so they forgot
and for all practical purposes
the idea ceased to exist.

But everyone has inside them
a plank and a screw
floating around.
Everyone is warm enough
to be alive.

102 Today

If Wystan Auden were alive today
he'd be a small tangle of black lines
on a rumpled white bedsheet,
his little eyes looking up at you.
What did you bring?
Some yellow daffodils and green stems.
Or did they bring you?

Auden once said,
"Where the hell is Bobby?"
and we looked around,
but there was no Bobby there.
Ah, Auden, no Bobby for you.
Just these daffodils in a clean white vase.

The Pounding Rabbit

After a clock designed by Neya Churyoku (1897–1987)

If you know the Japanese folktale
about the rabbit that ended up
on the moon, you will not be puzzled
by a table clock depicting a rabbit
pounding rice cakes on the moon,
but if you do not know this story
you will look at the clock and pound
your own head in disbelief,
as if to knock from it the spirit
you wish to offer to the gods
who munch the rice cakes
and never turn to say thank you
except by sending down a genius
to create such a clock, such a rabbit.

Mountains and Songs

Mountains of song
exert their force up through the earth
and rise above it

Peasants and villagers
cling to it as it rises
and they sing

and then they don't
for this is a pause
in the history of the world

and its mountains and songs

I saw them rising
and I knew it was weeping
this rising

for the mountains were going away
the villagers and peasants too
folded away in cupboards

in mountains and songs

It All Depends

Que reste-t-il de nos amours?
—CHARLES TRENET

Et nos amours, faut-il qu'il m'en souvienne?
—APOLLINAIRE

But it is not love that I would speak of
for as you see, I am of
the nineteenth century, when love was
. . . well, it all depends,
and I can't get out of it,
whatever this love is.
I will die in it and I hope
of it, it is the preamble
to walking in and sitting
down and saying "Hi"
before anything else has a chance
to happen. And then
of course nothing does,
which is why you keep saying it—
you can't get out
of saying it. So you may as well
take off your hat and stay a while,
which is what you always planned on anyway.

The nineteenth century,
what a tremendous thing
to be in love in!
Cottages go by
and music piles up

like excited dead people.
They stop but don't,
like sleeping people who are alive,
but it's not that easy,
the century is more complicated
than one had expected
now that everyone has a pot and a pan
but not a love of the pot and the pan.
Still, look at those sailing ships
on the wide main and the stairways
that spiral into heaven
and that bird with a long red beard
sticking straight up!
It's our chance to separate ourselves
into numerous pieces and have them
go in different directions,
reassembling what time had dispersed
in the form of granules and mist.
Or was it even really there?
A nightingale warbled
the tune it was supposed to
so the world would calm down.

There's nothing wrong with resting
alongside this shady rill and taking medications
as if they were piles of stones placed at intervals
by people who must have had a meaning
in mind but with no thought of telling you
what it was, for they didn't know that you
would exist. Therefore, lie down and rest.
The afternoon is mild and your love
is not driving you crazy, temporarily.

A rest might give you the strength
to look love straight in the eye
and not fade into granules and mist.

Reverdy said
"One must try to live"—
the statement of a man
who didn't love
or wasn't loved
enough. A small rectangle
of light lay on his floor
and his shoe
flashed as it went by.
His wife was hidden
in the kitchen, his girlfriend
hidden in celebrity,
his God just hidden.
Pierre opened the kitchen door,
the trap door of fame,
and the side of the cathedral,
but there was nothing there,
and when he opened his heart
he found only a rectangle
of sunlight on the floor.
But it was enough.

Perhaps his wife was hiding
her love in the kitchen,
the dark kitchen in Solesmes,
where I saw her walking
briskly down the street

at the age of 97 or 98,
the same street
a few years later
she would move slowly up
and down the way
to lie down in the tomb
next to Pierre, her Pierre.

By then the girlfriend
had twirled into Eternity,
and God had hidden so deeply
in Pierre's poems
Pierre didn't know
He was there—
He had gone back and disappeared
beneath the period
that ended Pierre's first book,
like a dark glint.
But God too was trying to live.

He hasn't been around lately,
which is perhaps why
the landscape is so cheerful—
it gets to be just itself,
brutally wonderfully so, and birds
veer and chirp and lift
their wings to see what's there.
It's air.
And so singing.

"But that's what *I* did,"
 says Pierre
 out of nowhere.
"And you can't tell
 if the singing made the air
 or the other way around—
 or both, which is most likely."
And then, like a Frenchman,
he left, before I had a chance
to throw him around the room,

but with respect,
affection, and mountains,
the kind they had in the century
he was born in, mountains as black
as his tomb, which I am unable
to throw around now
that his wife's in there too.

Henriette: her name.
(Henri: his real first name.)
(Her name a little feminine version of his.)
(But we all get smaller and smaller.)
(Hoping to fit
inside a rectangle of sunlight.)
(And not be a shoe!)
(Though have the calmness of a shoe.)
(Beneath the bed at night.)

I will tell you this tonight.

The Elevation of Ideals

To construct a set of ideals, a toy tool kit suffices, provided that the handles of the hammer, saw, and screwdriver are of wood and painted light blue. However, a full set of adult tools enables the builder to work more rapidly and with greater precision. Of equal importance are the raw materials, though it is possible to use various bits and pieces that one finds along the way. Remember, though, never to use metaphors in the construction, for over time they will shift, and the entire construction will sag and perhaps collapse. (Of course these rules apply only if you live on dry land; another set covers undersea construction.)

(If you end one ideal in parentheses, you must begin the next also in parentheses. Otherwise, the joint will not bond.) To construct a solid set of ideals, do not begin too early, for all too often the ideals do not turn out to be ideals at all: they are ideas, and, like bubbles, they tend to float away and pop. In doing so they can be beautiful, but æsthetic beauty is not of great importance here, unless it happens to be the same as moral beauty, which happens very rarely in modern societies. So allow your ideals to evolve through the decades. If you cherish them and don't think about them too much, they will change themselves by rotating on their axes while flashing on and off, to show you that all is well. When you turn fifty, they stop flashing, and for a while you think they have vanished, but it is you who have vanished, so thoroughly that even you do not know you are there. But you are.

You are, the way your mother is there, and your father, too. At this point you can obtain a set of tools and start thinking about the construction, how to begin it and where. These choices will be up to you: some choose the head, some the heart, and others even elect to build it outside themselves. The choice of location might bedevil you, but I will tell you now that the location doesn't really matter, except to you.

Deciding on the design of the construction can prove extremely difficult. This is normal, so don't fret about it. Just pick up the first ideal and see how it feels in your hand, then pick up a tool in the other hand. You will know immediately if they match. If they don't, try others. If nothing seems to work, you are not really fifty, and it is best to put the tools away and try later.

But do not postpone the resumption too long, for you might have grown so old that you no longer remember your project, or you may not be physically strong enough to make difficult moral decisions. Assuming, however, that you do resume, aim to build a perfect structure, no matter how small, for if the one you do complete is good enough it will float up of its own accord and stop in midair, where you can sing to it any time you want. If a door or window falls off, do not be concerned. Another door or window will appear in its place. And anyway, you will be inside, looking out.

Birgitte Hohlenberg

for Bill Berkson

I do not know who Birgitte Hohlenberg was
or why C. A. Jensen painted her portrait, in 1826,
but I'm glad he did, because then I could see it
in the Statens Museum for Kunst in Copenhagen
and buy a postcard of it and send it to my wife:
"Isn't she beautiful?" She being
Birgitte Hohlenberg *and* the painting of her.
I don't know which of them I love more.
Both are bright, calm, and sweet—
she had a way with beauty. You see it
in the brown satin dress with fluffy sleeves
and big white collar edged in lace, the hat
a light white puff around her head
and neatly tied beneath the chin,
her curly chestnut hair an echo
of the ribbon curling around the brim
and returning over the shoulders
to a loose knot at the collarbone,
her slender neck rising to a face whose high color elevates
how interested she is to be sitting there
looking straight at you without the slightest hint of carnality.
Just being in her presence would be enough
for me, now, at my age.
When did I send this card? August 15,
2001. That long ago. Before the Towers came down—
before a lot of things came down. But she

has stayed up, on my wife's dresser. How
she died I don't know, or at what age.
C. A. Jensen lived to 78, a long life
back then. Good for him.
I hope he was as happy
as he makes me every time I see his picture.
I hope you see it too.

Pep Talk

Dinner is a damned nice thing
as are breakfast and lunch
when they're good and with
the one you love.
That's a kind of dancing
sitting down and not moving
but what dances exactly
we do not know nor
need to know,
it is dancing us around
and nothing is moving
in the miracle of dinner
breakfast and lunch
and all the in-betweens
that give us pep.

Preface to Philosophy

An ugly day it must have been, when the first man stood face to face with the idea of the worthlessness and absurdity of life.
—W. MACNEILE DIXON

But it wasn't such an ugly day when I read Dixon's remark, at the age of fifteen, because I had already been *charmed* by the idea of the worthlessness and absurdity of life, which seemed far more sophisticated than the idea that life is meaningful and wonderful.

Now as I read it again for the first time in fifty-four years, what strikes me is not the truth of his statement, but the image of an early man's finding himself "face to face" with an idea; that is, with a ghostly being three times his size, wavering before him and communicating without speaking. Of course this is not what Dixon meant to convey; he was using "face to face" metaphorically, as an expressive device. But now I am face to face with his metaphor.

However, I can escape it by trying to picture the room in which I first read his remark, my bedroom, with its front window and side window. Sitting at my desk, I could have gazed out the front window and across the street to the window of my friend, from whom I had bought the book in which Dixon's writing appears, but if I was propped up in bed I could not have seen out the window directly behind me, whose curtain I usually kept drawn so that anyone stepping onto our porch would not glance in and see the back of my head. I did not want anyone to look at the back of my head.

As for its having been an ugly day, who knows? That is, "ugly" meaning what? Stormy? Dark? Probably the latter. Again he is speaking metaphorically, referring here to the psychological weather of the human nearly struck down by an idea, as I am struck, though not down, by the idea of a dark cloud in a protohuman shape fifteen feet high that descended and stood before the man and emanated the idea of the worthlessness and absurdity of life.

What made the man believe it? And then go on, as I have gone on?

You Know What

Every once in a while
it occurs to me
that I am a vibration
as hard as a living creature
and that that creature is me.
It occurs when I look out of my eyes
at it and it skulks away
into the dark area.

But you know what?
Take your philosophy
and put it in a paper bag
and carry it to a destination
and open it and see
if it looks back at you
and if it does
then you are occurring
because it is occurring too.

I learned that in my childhood
and I did have a childhood it was better than most
but I got nervous
when my mother got nervous
and my father was always quietly nervous.
We were a bundle of secret nerves sometimes
and at others we had quite a good time
especially my mother and me.
We would sing duets in the car

in harmony.
Sometimes she'd take the alto sometimes I would.
It was oddly satisfying
to come to a stop sign
and stop.

Lithuania
wasn't something I had heard of
and Stalin was I thought a cartoon character
because he had only one name and a mustache.
No one in America had a mustache
because Hitler had had one and he
wasn't funny he was shouting
and shaking his face around a tight nervous fit.
Our family was a little nervous but not like that.
He had a real problem we had a slight one.

One day someone told me to relax.
I didn't know what they meant,
I thought we were just the way we were.
We had names and identities and we knew
who each other was and what to say.
So what is "relaxing"? It is turning
into someone else in your own body
which is what is happening every moment anyway
but so slowly we can't see it—
in effect it isn't occurring
though really it is.

A Bit about Bishop Berkeley

Bishop Berkeley
is fond of saying,
in the middle of making a point,
"This is obvious
to anyone who takes a moment
to examine it with an attentive mind."
Then he says
"Abstract ideas do not exist,"
which sounds odd
until you see what he means
by *abstract*
and remember that he says
that language makes everything unclear,
though we need it
to get what we want.
He convinced investors
to give him a tidy sum
to open a school for colonial
and Native American children,
but the final funding fell through
so he bought Rhode Island
or a chunk of it
and went back to England
and told his investors,
"Abstract ideas do not exist."
This is obvious.
And oh, his name was George.

The Step Theory

An idea went by like a bird
and a bird went by like a cloud
and a cloud went by like a moment:
this is the Step Theory of Reality
and its by-product the Ziggurat Configuration.
Then a bird went by like an idea—
the idea of the Step Theory itself,
for no one thinks of it anymore,
because its pieces lock together seamlessly,
the way a play on words
is just words and not just words
at the same time, for a moment.
It can't come back
because it never went anywhere,
unlike a cloud that can't come back
because it went everywhere.
And so we jump around and sputter,
to the great amusement
of our higher selves,
the ones we can't find,
their laughter echoing forever
in the few moments we have.

That's step 1.
Now sweep idea, bird, and cloud
into a little pile and put them in a box.
(They will come in handy later.)

For step 2 you must forget
who you aren't, that is,
everyone else, even though you
are part everyone else.
This in itself is not difficult:
you do it all the time
when you're not looking.
What *is* difficult is what follows:
you must make yourself
as flat as a pancake
and try to avoid having syrup
poured onto you.
Most people will not
pour syrup onto a human pancake,
but there are a few who would.
Once you are flat, just lie there
for a while. Look at those clouds
and the bird that flew into the idea of them.

Eventually the Ziggurat Configuration
comes into play. The weather is hot and humid
but the ziggurat keeps climbing itself
until it gets to the top, then
it comes back down, only to climb back up,
and so on. I once had an aunt like this
—there was no stopping her—
her face in profile formed a ziggurat.
We children put glasses of water
on the steps, thus representing the soul
without knowing that it takes a while
to learn that we have one, but

by that time the soul had vanished
into the process of being itself,
like the idea, the bird, and the cloud:
song, song, and song.

Step 3 is for later,
but I can tell you now
that it involves rolling green pastureland
you step into but not onto
and follow your nose,
no cloud, no bird, no idea.

My '75 Chevy

Out in the yard
sits my 1975 Chevy pickup truck,
repainted red with a white roof,
body smooth, carburetor rebuilt, new tires,
new dashboard, black leather seat covers,
new floorboards, and two new side mirrors.
In a timeless yard—
it creates its own time zone. 1975.
I can't drive simultaneously in 1975 and 2012,
but I do
because when the truck goes forward
I enter the sliding zone known
as Miles Per Hour
and I'm just someone in something red.

For A.

The little blue heron's back again
Was he here when
Joe was here too
with Bill and me and you
when we were all just fifty?
If the three of us add twenty
we'll get something unreal
unlike what we are and feel
which is what Joe
couldn't imagine and ever know:
how my grandma said now and then
"I'm in good shape for the shape I'm in."

Art Lessons

Narrative Painting

The Madonna never walks.

The Portrait

Bronzino did for the portrait what the portrait did for the sitter.

Still Life

The best still lifes have emptiness.

The Self-Portrait

The self-portrait did for the self what the self did for the portrait.

Landscape

Landscape is a window through which you see what you thought.

Sculpture

Don't move.

A Few Ideas about Rabbits

It's hard to understand what
a rabbit is

It lifts a paw
and hesitates

For a moment its nose
and mouth are all cat

and those eyes, so worried
so harmless

but it might scratch you
accidentally

and that camel back
and tiger crouch

ears of lemur
perked up

Mouse-kangaroo

The rabbit runs around
eating and doing arithmetic

There is the story of the grateful king
who offered his subject anything

he wanted, and the subject said
Take this chessboard and put

a coin on the first square
then double that amount for the second

and so on, to which the king
readily consented

and when they counted
it turned out to be

a billion trillion coins
(or something like that)

more than the richest king
could afford

Imagine if the man had asked
for rabbits

Well that's what Nature asked for.
In Australia I think

there's an area that has
ten rabbits per square yard

Ah, we must shoot them
cry certain Australians

and others say No
ship them to a place

that has no rabbits
But there's a reason

there are no rabbits there
like at the North Pole

or in the Gobi Desert
or on Park Avenue

Anyway I do not trust a rabbit
because I have no idea

what it is thinking
I trust a worm because it isn't thinking

If rabbits could say
"I will hop into this garden

and eat the lettuce"
I would like them more

The Value of Discipline

I am very disappointed in you, Myron.
You are a very smart boy,
 and we had high hopes for you.
But now this.
I don't know.
Go to your room.

Myron heads toward his room,
but does his head hang low?
No way!
He is looking straight ahead
and feeling a hot black liquid
trickle through his heart.

Great galleons
bound through the rough seas
and on them bearded men
are shouting sailor things
as if to the wind.

Back in his room
the objects look older.
What joy to make them
walk the plank!
Avast! Avaunt! Splash! Garrrr!

Pea Jacket

Years ago I had an old pea jacket
Slightly scruffy but not unclean
was my overall look and I lacked
the easy assurance that comes with money
because I had very little

It was okay, not having money
I wasn't starving or lacking anything I needed
though by contemporary standards
I should have been envious or angry
I wasn't
All I cared about was my wife and friends and family
Books writing perception great art and gigantic metaphysical
    questions floating in on good humor
Society could take care of itself more or less
(It turned out less)
and I was happy enough and eager
I think what I mean is I was young
so that no matter what anyone might think of my jacket
I liked it it fit well and was warm in the New York winter
collar turned up and hands snug in pockets

It came from a secondhand clothing store
at the corner of Bowery and Bleecker maybe it
had belonged to a drunken sailor
What do you do with a drunken sailor early in the morning?
Put him in bed with the captain's daughter!

There was a label inside with his name and serial number scrawled on it
It felt odd wearing his name I snipped it out

I don't have anything monumental or metaphoric to say about my jacket
It's just a pleasure to remember it and how good it felt on me
Then one day I started wearing something else
and a few years later I gave the jacket to someone I liked I don't recall who

The Ukrainian Museum

Just walking into the new and beautifully designed Ukrainian Museum was a pleasure: varnished hardwood floors, white walls, clean lines, understated lighting, and the luxury of newness. An older Ukrainian Museum had been located in a second-floor apartment in a tenement building on Second Avenue, without even a sign outside, several rooms of dismal paintings in drab light; the one time I ventured in, there was not a single soul in the place, not even a guard. Twenty years later the museum moved a few blocks up the street to a space protected by two security checkpoints. I was greeted, if that is the word, by a woman who coldly asked me what I wanted. The two exhibition rooms were slightly larger than closets. Now, walking into this third incarnation made me feel so light and carefree that I had to be reminded to buy a ticket.

The Alexander Archipenko exhibition was the largest I had ever seen of his work, and as I moved from sculpture to sculpture I felt grateful just to be there. But I wasn't really "there," I was in a wholesale meat market. The smell of raw flesh and gore oozes out the ramshackle front doors where trucks have backed up to disgorge sides of beef and pork. Just inside are butchers in threadbare aprons streaked with blood. One of them waddles his mammoth girth toward me, a cigarette dangling from his pudgy lips, a strange leer on his face. He is the one who lewdly propositioned a friend of mine who lives a few doors away. Nineteen sixty-one.

Now, in 2005, I am walking through this museum on the very spot where those butchers slashed and chopped up carcasses. The fat one is no doubt dead, like my friend and Archipenko. The exhibition is fine, but I can't focus on it, so I simply pause before each piece.

Finally I can't restrain myself from approaching someone, who happened to be a guard, an Indian or Pakistani woman, to whom I say, "Many years ago, when I first came to New York, I had a friend who lived a few doors down the street. Do you know what this place was then? It was a wholesale meat business." She looks at me and says, "Yes, it's amazing the way they change things so fast," and looks away.

The 1870s

Homage to Michel Butor

1870 Work on Brooklyn Bridge begun. Charles Dickens dies. Jules Verne writes *20,000 Leagues under the Sea*. Rockefeller founds Standard Oil. Robert E. Lee dies.

1871 British Columbia joins Canada. Marcel Proust born. Rasputin born. Pneumatic rock drill invented. Stanley meets Livingstone. Whistler paints *The Artist's Mother*. The Great Fire of Chicago. P. T. Barnum opens "The Greatest Show on Earth."

1872 Jesuits expelled from Germany. Grant reelected President. Bertrand Russell born. First operation on the esophagus. Piet Mondrian born.

1873 New York financial panic. Germans evacuate France. First color photograph. Zanzibar abolishes slave trade. E. Remington & Sons, gunsmiths, produce typewriters. Tolstoy writes *Anna Karenina*. Buda and Pest unite.

1874 Winston Churchill born. Gertrude Stein born. First roller-skating rink. First Impressionist exhibition. Pressure cooking invented. Thomas Hardy writes *Far from the Madding Crowd*. First ice cream soda.

1875 Carl Jung born. Thomas Mann born. Rainer Maria Rilke born. Maurice Ravel born. Madam Blavatsky founds Theosophical Society. Camille Corot dies. Georges Bizet dies. Hans Christian Andersen dies. First swim across the English Channel.

1876 Korea becomes a nation. Brahms composes Symphony no. 1. Turks massacre Bulgarians. Pablo Casals born. George Sand dies. Bruno Walter born. Carpet sweeper invented. Degas paints *The Glass of Absinthe.*

1877 Edison invents the phonograph. Gustave Courbet dies. Queen Victoria becomes Empress of India. First contact lenses. Canals on Mars observed. First public telephones in the U.S.

1878 Greece declares war on Turkey. Hughes invents the microphone. Mannlicher invents the repeater rifle. W. A. Burpee does something with Burpee seeds.

1879 British/Zulu War. Joseph Stalin born. Albert Einstein born. Discovery of saccharin. First public telephones in London. Paul Cézanne paints *Self-Portrait.* Edison has an idea and invents the light bulb.

One Thing Led to Another

If it wasn't one thing
it was another.
You can't believe
how charged everything is
with meaning
because it is meaningless.
Joy in the curtains,
the farmer in the dell,
a fellow named
whatever it was—Floyd?
And then you had arms and legs
and it wasn't funny.
It was a freshly baked pie.
I could care
more or less.
Like a machine
in the heavens, shooting,
or an exclamation point
in the motion picture industry.
Cut.
It's always something.
"Tuck in your shirt"
is not said to a dog.
What's the use of whining?
No one really enjoys it.

The Rabbi with a Puzzle Voice

Wait a minute
I forgot something
The rabbi with a puzzle voice
Pieces flying around in the air
Texas Lithuania and now another one
A rectangle
He is singing them

I always knew he was
And the song is oh
I don't really know what
Very old like a doughnut
And a look through its hole
But he is singing
And that's the main thing, no?

The other main thing
Is that you're on that rectangle
Floating to the ground
As it loses its oomph
And other shapes are flying out above you
And you are on them too!
How can this be?

It is part of the jigsaw puzzle
And the sad voice that created it
Why did you have to be anyone
Whoever you are

Is what the rabbi sings
Whoever he is
Maybe he's not a rabbi at all

There was a reason I had forgotten him
And a reason I remember him
And his puzzle voice
But where are his edges going
As now he too breaks into pieces
Pieces pieces
That arc out in his song

Syntactical Structures

It was as if
while I was driving down a one-lane dirt road
with tall pines on both sides
the landscape had a syntax
similar to that of our language
and as I moved along
a long sentence was being spoken
on the right and another on the left
and I thought
Maybe the landscape
can understand what I say too.
Ahead was a farmhouse
with children playing near the road
so I slowed down
and waved to them.   ·
They were young enough
to smile and wave back.

The World of Us

Who was the first person to say
"I think the world of you"
and how did he or she come up with it?
It's the kind of thing
one ascribes to a god
or a great philosopher
or a lunatic
on a good day. Now
it's a cliché
because we can't think it,
we can only hear ourselves saying it.

There are a lot of things we can't think
or don't want to. It's hard
for example
to think of skin as an organ
—an organ is a kidney or a musical instrument
or even a publication—
but ask any doctor
and the doctor will say
"Yes, the skin is an organ."
Imagine having that organ removed
(being skinned alive)
or rather don't
at least not too vividly.
It's better to keep a barrier
between oneself and things
that can be horrendous
like life.

Don't go around all day
thinking about life—
doing so will raise a barrier
between you and its instants.
You need those instants
so you can be in them,
and I need you to be in them with me
for I think the world of us
and the mysterious barricades
that make it possible.

But you say
"First you say to raise a barrier
and then not to."
Yes, because these
are two different barriers,
one a barrier against life,
the other a barrier against being alive.
Being alive is good, life is bad.

"So, what about being dead?
Is that bad?
And what about heaven?"
I don't know about being dead
because I can't remember what it was like,
but I do know
that it is awful and amusing to be part heaven
and not know which part of you it is.
Unless you don't think about it,
in which case
you find yourself looking up and saying

"That is *the* best cornbread I've ever eaten."
Along with it comes a yawn at the end of a long and satisfying day,
everything quiet and thrilling
inside a consciousness surrounded by a night
in which exclamation marks are flying toward a single point.

Curtain

Standing in the bathroom peeing
I look up at the curtain in front of me
red cotton with little yellow flowers
from Liberty Fabrics (London) 1970
and I feel I am flying up into the heavens
until I remember that soon
I will turn 70 and at any moment
I could feel a sudden paroxysmal pain
in my head and with the curtain
dropping away fall over dead—
this could happen right now!
But it doesn't, the curtain stays put
and I'm standing there
and the curtain still looks good.

Homage to Meister Eckhart

I promised myself
I would explore my void
the space I occupy
and won't
but I'm still waiting

waiting

waiting in a room
for the room to change into an idea a flower might have

The sun shines down on the flower
in the idea the flower does have at all times

and at all times you hear its thudding
and in between the thuds
is a silence in which a thud almost is

The first time I heard the word *void*
it was from the Bible: "And the earth
was without form and void."
I was a child. I thought it meant
the earth was without void.
Which meant nothing to me
because I did not know the meaning of *void*.
And I didn't know there was a comma
that changes everything:

"was without form, and void."
The cosmos changed by a comma!

Years later a big face with no features
came out of the trees in the night
and said, brutally, "Void"
as if handing me a gift

I opened my eyes and there it was
in the mirror it was I or something else
I wasn't sure
but I was happy to be in between
My soul was growing up
It had learned how to put quotation marks
around everything

which destroyed everything
to make two of everything
one for each eye and one for each ear

but the eyes get further and further apart
from what they see
as the ears get closer and closer
to what they hear
like the dot terribly far away
and big in front of your face
at the same time and loud

So move
the mirror
the Void

into another mirror
or Void
and just let go

But the eyes eventually alight
on words like SPONGEBOB SQUAREPANTS
printed on the side
of everyone's head
the way CLEM KADIDDLEHOPPER used to be
and MEISTER ECKHART and MAX JACOB
all appearing nightly
in a revue set in the void of heaven,
the void that allowed God to be there
as the sole spectator
until your void and his void were almost the same
as the void of Spongebob and Max, Clem too,
but not quite, for, as Eckhart says,
"The nothingness of God fills all things
while his somethingness is nowhere"
and so "The very best thing you can do
is to remain still for as long as possible"
and wait for the nothingness of God.

The Incoherent Behavior of Most Lawn Furniture

Suddenly the lawn furniture moves to different spots and stops, overturned or sideways on the ground or hovering in the air, then the pieces jerk, flip, or fly into new spots, in no pattern or rhythm. But the wooden fold-up lawn chair, with its wide strip of canvas forming a gentle sling from top to bottom, remains still. Its striped pattern ripples in the breeze, and though its wooden frame eventually turns gray it never rots or breaks, no matter how inclement the weather. Over the years, however, this lawn chair slowly grows less and less visible, so slowly that no one notices, until it disappears. It remains there, unseen and lost to memory, until one day someone remembers its green and orange stripes, its welcoming curve, its simplicity, there in the sunlight.

This Schoolhouse Look

is rather cute, no? This

is how I always wanted to have my writing look

It has the charm

of the desire for perfection

that I had

when I had the charm

of not knowing better

if you can call it charm

I wanted to do better

without knowing anything

I still do

The Street

The last time I came back to New York I didn't know
that it would be the last time you'd be here
though you *are* still here in the form of you
who a block away walk toward me until it *isn't* you,
it's someone with a fine head and silver hair and blue eyes
and the suggestion of not being like anyone else
and it's you I'm waiting for as I walk past Little Poland
or come out of New York Central Art Supply or stop to look
at the poppy seed cake in the window of Baczynsky's on Second Avenue,
the cake I brought up to your place sometimes
when we were working together and you'd say "Tea?"
as if it were spelled with only the one letter.

Knowing you were there made me be more here too,
made New York be New York,
fueled my anger at the new buildings that ruined the old ones
and at the new people with their coarseness and self-involvement
you avoided by going out to buy the *Times* at 5 a.m.,
then came back and made yourself a pot of espresso
and read the paper as if you were in Tuscany
which is where you soon will be
in that niche in the wall all ten pounds of you
and I'll leave the city that's slipped a little further away no a lot.

Paris Again

I'm afraid of the thrill of touching you again
and seeing you appear before my eyes
because you are beautiful the way things used to be.

One day I sat down in a café and ordered an *accent aigu*
and a *citron pressé* and looked at Paris.
I said to myself This is Paris and you
are in it so you are Paris too. *Garçon,*
encore un accent aigu s'il vous plaît
but he didn't look pleased he was Parisian.
Maybe I too could learn how to be grumpy
and snooty and Cartesian and quick all at the same time.

The Nord-Sud metro line ran all the way
from the tips of my toes to the top of my head
where it paused and went down again
and every time it went past Odéon I thought
of Reverdy and how grumpy
and suddenly fiery he could be and figured
he would have no patience with a guy like me
who had a touch of Max Jacob ready
to leap up and turn an angel into a sad witticism
about the God Pierre was wrestling with as if
they were both made of granite. But they weren't.
And neither was I, like those who love and have loved
and are still afraid of the thrill of the beauty of everything that is gone.

London, 1815

We go clippety-clop
because we are horseshoes
on cobblestones. O
to be a houseshoe
in a house
and resting comfortably
alongside another houseshoe!
But the horse clops on,
our echos echoing
down a dark alley
behind a dark house.

Of Copse and Coppice

When asked
if I knew the meaning
of the word *copse* c-o-p-s-e
I said "Of course, it means . . .
I think it means a field
or meadow." One
of the first poems
I ever wrote said
"Where is the copse
with verdant green?"
because at age thirteen
I wanted to use
words new to me.
Now *copse* is new again
because I'm now not sure
just what it means.
A *coppice* is a thicket,
no?

    Oh you're such
    an American! out
    of touch
    with the natural world
    and English English
    and your own adolescence
    all at the same time!
    Alas, I've wandered
    lonely as a crowd

of words
blown down the street
this way and that,
vagabond lexicon
dressed as a citizen.

    Maybe a wood or a grove?
    I've always liked
    my grandfather's name Grover
    and one of the most beautiful girls
    of my adolescence was named
    Madeleine Grove
    and back then
    my favorite publisher was Grove.
    Shady Grove, my true love
    the song goes. Them
    I remember. *Copse*
    and *coppice* are phonemes
    from literature. I preferred
    cops and robbers.

    But it got better.
    I nabbed the robbers
    and shot a few Indians
    clean out of their saddles
    but they didn't have saddles
    and weren't even Indians
    and it didn't matter:
    you had to go
    and in a few minutes
    I did too,

due as I was
in this verdant copse
splashed with shadows
that shift and wave like plaid
in the wind from off the brae.

Manifestation and Mustache

I love living here
away from a lot of things
that annoy me
and close to a lot
of things I love
like air like trees
and emptiness.
But the thing
I love best
goes where I go
and will go with me
when I am gone
from where I am
and into
where love
doesn't figure,
which I have done
a few times
in my life,
if memory serves.
Then
the mustache
comes in
and says,
"You can't be right
and wrong
at the same time,"
but I don't believe it.

Shipwreck in General

Is there no end to anything ever

I release the question mark
From its tether and it floats
Like a life jacket
In search of the shipwreck
That every question is

But today it finds no victim
No flotsam no captain's cap
For today is shipwreck-free it is
The end of shipwreck in general
And the curl and the dot below
Can go their separate ways
And be whatever they like

French Art in the 1950s

Ronnie is finding out about art in the 1950s. He is learning that it had a palette and brushes and colors, and the palette had a hole, in which the brushes were inserted and where they seemed debonnaire and ready to do something but also happy not to. There is an artist in the room. He wears a smock and a beret, and he has a pencil mustache. His name is Pierre, for he is French. Art comes from France. Pierre is going to bring some more of it to us. But at the moment he is thinking about what he is going to paint today. A pear? A young woman who is wearing no clothing? Or perhaps just a lot of colors flying around on the canvas, to represent his feelings?

But wait, it is time for lunch. Later in the afternoon he will execute his picture. For now he must go to the café and greet his admirers, who, on seeing him, call out "Pierre!" and "Over here, Pierre!" and, cleverly, "There he is, the rascal!" But everyone knows that Pierre is not a rascal. He is a French artist. You can tell by the smock he has forgotten to remove. Later, when it has paint smears and spots on it, even an imbecile will be able to see that he is an artist. Ronnie already knows.

Three Poems in Honor of Willem de Kooning

I Felt

For a moment
as if I were talking to you
and you were listening
and taking me seriously
the way a grandfather does
when he's open and kind,
you knew what
was troubling me
and you knew
that the best thing to do
was to listen
and say nothing,
allowing a calm to settle
into the grandfather
that turns out to be me.

The Door to the River

You walked through it before
you even knew it was there

The river came up to the door
and asked to come in

Then the river came through the door
and the door floated away

I once threw away a river
because it looked old enough

And I bought a new one
and a door along with it

Except it never was a door
It was a doorway

Like Norway
with windows

Zot

In de Kooning's painting, the word *zot*.
I thought *sot?*
Then learned that *zot*
is Dutch for *foolish*. So
foolish and *drunk* swirled around
and separated out
into the Dutch *foolish* and the English *drunk*.
He wasn't such a big drinker
when he did that painting,
but maybe he felt like a fool sometimes
—of course he did.
He was *zot* and he knew it
and he told you so, you
being almost nobody,
so almost nobody you were
even more *zot* than he!
Zot is vat I tink.

Alone and Not Alone

Out of the water
came the one
who reached back
into the water
and pulled out the zero.

The time is now.

The time is now 8:15 p.m.
Eastern Standard Time.

In Beijing Lan Lan
is getting up
tomorrow.
I see her pretty, smiling face
as she curls back the covers.

Tonight I
will get under the covers
and think of her face
not because I
am in love with her
but because I
like her face
though I
do not want it
on my head.

Out of the water
came my head,
head first, whoosh!
A person's head
does not belong
underwater.

Look at fish!
Who wants to be one?

I would
for a moment
or two. Then
back to me.

It would be terrible
to alternate
being fish
and person
every few seconds.

We inhale
then exhale
every few seconds.

Lan Lan's
two daughters
are inhaling and exhaling,
still asleep—
it is Sunday
in Beijing.

Lan Lan's husband
is sitting at a table
in the kitchen
thinking
about the poetry
of Alexander Blok.

Alexander Blok
is pouring hot water
into the teapot.
Out of the water
came the tea
and out of the tea
came the scent of jasmine.

And then Alexander Blok
was not there.
He had to go away
and die again.

He exhaled and then
exhaled, and then
was like a dead fish,
wrapped in a newspaper
whose headline says
BLOK DEAD.
He reached back
and pulled himself
out of life
and into those two words.

Lan Lan's husband
looks up confused—
his mind is in Russian
but everything else
is in Chinese
when she comes in
and the jasmine is deeper
and more of you now.

It is 8:33.
What happened?

You were not alone
in thinking you were alone.

COFFEE HOUSE PRESS

The mission of Coffee House Press is to publish exciting, vital, and enduring authors of our time; to delight and inspire readers; to contribute to the cultural life of our community; and to enrich our literary heritage. By building on the best traditions of publishing and the book arts, we produce books that celebrate imagination, innovation in the craft of writing, and the many authentic voices of the American experience.

Visit us at coffeehousepress.org.

Funder Acknowledgments

Coffee House Press is an independent, nonprofit literary publisher. All of our books, including the one in your hands, are made possible through the generous support of grants and donations from corporate giving programs, state and federal support, family foundations, and the many individuals that believe in the transformational power of literature. We receive major operating support from Amazon, the Bush Foundation, the McKnight Foundation, the National Endowment for the Arts—a federal agency, and Target. This activity is made possible by the voters of Minnesota through a Minnesota State Arts Board Operating Support grant, thanks to a legislative appropriation from the arts and cultural heritage fund.

Coffee House Press receives additional support from many anonymous donors; the Alexander Family Fund; the Archer Bondarenko Munificence Fund; the Elmer L. & Eleanor J. Andersen Foundation; the David & Mary Anderson Family Foundation; the W. & R. Bernheimer Family Foundation; the E. Thomas Binger & Rebecca Rand Fund of the Minneapolis Foundation; the Patrick & Aimee Butler Family Foundation; the Buuck Family Foundation; the Carolyn Foundation; Dorsey & Whitney Foundation; Fredrikson & Byron, P.A.; the Jerome Foundation; the Lenfestey Family Foundation; the Mead Witter Foundation; the Nash Foundation; the Rehael Fund of the Minneapolis Foundation; the Schwab Charitable Fund; Schwegman, Lundberg & Woessner, P.A.; Penguin Group; the Private Client Reserve of US Bank; VSA Minnesota for the Metropolitan Regional Arts Council; the Archie D. & Bertha H. Walker Foundation; the Wells Fargo Foundation of Minnesota; and the Woessner Freeman Family Foundation.

The Publisher's Circle of Coffee House Press

Publisher's Circle members make significant contributions to Coffee House Press's annual giving campaign. Understanding that a strong financial base is necessary for the press to meet the challenges and opportunities that arise each year, this group plays a crucial part in the success of our mission.

"Coffee House Press believes that American literature should be as diverse as America itself. Known for consistently championing authors whose work challenges cultural and æsthetic norms, we believe their books deserve space in the marketplace of ideas. Publishing literature has never been an easy business, and publishing literature that truly takes risks is a cause we believe is worthy of significant support. We ask you to join us today in helping to ensure the future of Coffee House Press."

—THE PUBLISHER'S CIRCLE MEMBERS
OF COFFEE HOUSE PRESS

PUBLISHER'S CIRCLE MEMBERS

Many Anonymous Donors
Mr. & Mrs. Rand L. Alexander
Suzanne Allen
Patricia Beithon
Bill Berkson & Connie Lewallen
Robert & Gail Buuck
Claire Casey
Louise Copeland
Jane Dalrymple-Hollo
Mary Ebert & Paul Stembler
Chris Fischbach & Katie Dublinski
Katharine Freeman

Sally French
Jocelyn Hale & Glenn Miller
Roger Hale & Nor Hall
Jeffrey Hom
Kenneth & Susan Kahn
Kenneth Koch Literary Estate
Stephen & Isabel Keating
Allan & Cinda Kornblum
Leslie Larson Maheras
Jim & Susan Lenfestey
Sarah Lutman & Rob Rudolph
Carol & Aaron Mack
George Mack
Joshua Mack
Gillian McCain
Mary & Malcolm McDermid
Sjur Midness & Briar Andresen
Peter Nelson & Jennifer Swenson
Marc Porter & James Hennessy
E. Thomas Binger & Rebecca Rand Fund of the Minneapolis
Foundation
Jeffrey Sugerman & Sarah Schultz
Nan Swid
Patricia Tilton
Stu Wilson & Melissa Barker
Warren D. Woessner & Iris C. Freeman
Margaret & Angus Wurtele

For more information about the Publisher's Circle and
other ways to support Coffee House Press books, authors,
and activities, please visit www.coffeehousepress.org/support
or contact us at: info@coffeehousepress.org.

Allan Kornblum, 1949–2014

Vision is about looking at the world and seeing
not what it is, but what it could be. Allan Kornblum's vision and
leadership created Coffee House Press. To celebrate his legacy,
every book we publish in 2015 will be in his memory.

Alone and Not Alone was designed at Coffee House Press, in the historic Grain Belt Brewery's Bottling House near downtown Minneapolis. The text is set in Adobe Garamond. Composition by Bookmobile Design & Digital Publisher Services, Minneapolis, Minnesota. Manufactured by Versa Press on acid-free paper.

RON PADGETT grew up in Tulsa and has lived mostly in New York City since 1960. Among his many honors are a Guggenheim Fellowship, the American Academy of Arts and Letters poetry award, the Shelley Memorial Award, and grants from the National Endowment for the Arts. Padgett's *How Long* was a Pulitzer Prize finalist in poetry and his *Collected Poems* won the William Carlos Williams Award from the Poetry Society of America and the Los Angeles Times Book Prize for the best poetry book of 2013. In addition to being a poet, he is a translator of Guillaume Apollinaire, Pierre Reverdy, and Blaise Cendrars. His own work has been translated into eighteen languages.

—